A

SICILIAN
C O O K B O O K

MARY MAW AND RADHA PATTERSON
Illustrated by PAULINE O'REILLY

APPLETREE PRESS

First published in 1995 by
The Appletree Press Ltd, 19–21 Alfred Street,
Belfast BT2 8DL
Tel. +44 (0) 1232 243074
Fax +44 (0) 1232 246756
Printed in the E.U. All rights reserved.
Copyright © The Appletree Press Ltd.

A Little Sicilian Cookbook

A catalogue record for this book is
available from the British Library.

ISBN 0-86281-537-1

9 8 7 6 5 4 3 2 1

A note on measures

Measurements are given in metric, imperial and American
measures. Spoon measurements are level.
Seasonings can be adjusted to taste.

Introduction

Sicily, largest of the Mediterranean islands, lies between Europe and Africa and its history, culture and food belong to both continents. The Greeks, Phoenicians, Romans, Arabs, Normans, Spanish and Italians have all laid claim to the island and each wave of invaders has left its mark on the island's food. Greeks and Romans brought grapes, olives wheat and cheese. The Arabs brought aubergines, artichokes, sugar cane, citrus fruits, almonds and pistachios. The Spanish introduced sweet peppers and, indirectly, were responsible for the now ubiquitous tomato. Under Spanish rule the island's aristocracy prospered and grew and, by the early nineteenth century, French cuisine was the style of cooking preferred by the upper classes.

For the rest of the population poverty was a fact of life. Traditional Sicilian food is based on what ingredients were readily and cheaply available. Pasta, central to the Sicilian diet, is dressed with a range of sauces based on fish and vegetables. Tuna, sardines and swordfish are the seafood most commonly eaten, and artichokes, aubergines, peppers and tomatoes are the favourite vegetables. Meat and chicken play only a small part in traditional Sicilian cooking, but cheeses are incorporated into many dishes.

It is the island's *dolci* (desserts) which are perhaps the greatest triumph of the Sicilian kitchen. *Cassata* and *cannoli* are irresistible and the ice creams made in Sicilian *gelaterie* are second to none.

Where possible we have chosen or adapted recipes which can be attempted without too much difficulty. Our selection offers, we hope, an introduction to the complexities of Sicilian cooking and the inspiration to explore further the food of this most fascinating Mediterranean island.

Street Food

Arancine di Riso

Arancine, which means "little oranges", are part of the Sicilian tradition of street food.

4oz/100g arborio rice	pinch of nutmeg
3oz/75g ricotta cheese, mashed	3oz/75g mozzarella cheese,
1oz/25g Parmesan or pecorino	chopped
cheese, grated	3 tbsp flour
bunch of parsley, finely chopped	3 tbsp fine breadcrumbs
2 eggs	vegetable oil for frying
salt and pepper	

Cook the rice in 1³/₄ pints/1 litre of water for about 15 minutes, until tender. Drain, spread out on a large plate and allow to cool. Put into a bowl and add the ricotta, the Parmesan or pecorino, parsley, one egg, salt, pepper and the nutmeg. Mix thoroughly and then add the chopped mozzarella. Shape the mixture into balls, using wet hands to prevent stickiness. Roll the balls first in flour, then in beaten egg and finally in breadcrumbs. Deep fry in oil until golden. Drain on absorbent paper and serve hot.

Panelle

Street food such as *panelle*, probably Arabian in origin, is still to be found in abundance in Palermo.

8oz/250g chick pea flour
1 pt/600ml/2¹/₂ cups water
salt and freshly ground black pepper
vegetable oil for frying

Pour the water into a thick-bottomed saucepan and add the chick pea flour in a steady stream, whisking constantly to prevent lumps. Add the salt and pepper and cook until it thickens. Remove from heat and pour the mixture onto a cold flat surface such as a baking sheet or a marble slab. As far as possible, form a rectangle less than 1/4 inch/1 cm thick. Leave to cool. When cold, cut the paste into small rectangles or triangles. Fry the *panelle* in about 2 inches/5cm of hot oil until both sides are golden brown. Drain on absorbent paper and serve at once.

Pasta con le Sarde

Pasta con le Sarde is one of the most famous and unique of all the island's pasta dishes. The combination of such Sicilian ingredients as wild fennel, raisins, pine nuts, breadcrumbs and sardines make this dish truly distinctive. Wild fennel is not always easily found but cultivated fennel makes an acceptable substitute, though the flavour is not so intense.

8–10 fresh sardines	*2oz/50g pine nuts*
2 tbsp seasoned flour	*1oz/25g raisins*
1 small onion, finely chopped	*12oz/350g spaghetti or penne*
olive oil	*4 tbsp breadcrumbs, toasted*
a good bunch of green	*in a frying pan*
fennel leaves	

Bone and clean the sardines, remove their heads and coat them with the seasoned flour. Fry the onions in a little olive oil until they are golden. Add the fennel and cook over a low heat. Put in the raisins and pine nuts and cook for a few minutes. Fry the sardines in olive oil and then set aside. Cook the pasta in plenty of salted, boiling water until *al dente*. Drain and stir in the fennel mixture. Arrange the sardines over the top and sprinkle with the toasted breadcrumbs just before serving.

Pasta alla Norma

One of Sicily's best known pasta dishes, said to be so named because it reaches the heights of perfection of the opera Norma written by the Sicilian-born composer, Bellini.

I large aubergine, sliced into rounds	I tsp sugar
	salt and pepper
8 fl oz/200ml/I cup olive oil	I lb/450g spaghettini
I small onion, finely chopped	4oz/100g/¹/₂ cup Parmesan or
2 cloves garlic, finely chopped	pecorino cheese
14oz/400g tin chopped tomatoes	a few basil leaves, roughly torn

Place the aubergine in a colander, sprinkle with salt and leave to disgorge for up to I hour. Put one tablespoon of olive oil and the onion in a saucepan and cook until soft. Add the garlic and cook for a few more minutes. Put in the tomatoes, sugar, salt and pepper, and cook for 20 minutes or so on a gentle heat until the sauce thickens. Dry the aubergines, heat the remaining olive oil in a frying pan, and when it is very hot, add the aubergine slices, a few at a time. Fry until golden on both sides and then place them on absorbent paper. Cook the spaghettini in plenty of salted boiling water, until it is *al dente*. Drain the pasta, place in a large bowl and dress with half the sauce and half the grated cheese. Top with the slices of aubergine and the rest of the tomato sauce. Finish with a sprinkling of cheese and the basil leaves and serve at once.

Pasta con Mollica e Acciughe

Breadcrumbs are an important part of Sicilian cooking. They are used for stuffing meat and fish and as a substitute for cheese on pizza or pasta. Anchovies are also used a great deal by Sicilian cooks and in this simple recipe these two ingredients are combined to create a dish rich in flavour and texture.

---

5 tbsp olive oil
3oz/75g/¹/₂ cup fresh breadcrumbs
2 cloves garlic, finely chopped
6–8 anchovy fillets
1 lb/450g spaghetti or spaghettini
1 tbsp parsley, finely chopped

To make the breadcrumbs for this dish, heat 2 tablespoons of olive oil in a frying pan and add the breadcrumbs. Stir over a moderate heat until the crumbs are brown and crisp. Put the remaining 3 tablespoons of olive oil in a saucepan with the finely chopped garlic and sauté until it begins to colour. Add the anchovy fillets and remove from the heat. The anchovies must not cook or they will become bitter. Cook the spaghettini in lots of boiling salted water and when *al dente* drain and put in a large bowl. Add the anchovy sauce, mix thoroughly, sprinkle with breadcrumbs and parsley and serve at once.

Pasta con il Tonno Rosso

It was Ignazio Florio, a Palermitano, who first thought of putting tuna in a tin and Sicilians now use tinned tuna to make flavoursome sauces for pasta. The ingredients for this recipe can be found in most larders and can be rustled up in no time at all.

---

4 tbsp olive oil
1 clove garlic, finely chopped
14oz/400g tin chopped tomatoes
pinch of sugar
salt and freshly ground black pepper
1 lb/450g spaghetti
11oz/300g tinned tuna (preferably packed in olive oil)
1 tbsp parsley, finely chopped

Put the olive oil and garlic in a sauté pan over a moderate heat and cook until garlic turns golden. Add tomatoes and their juice, sugar, salt and pepper. Simmer gently for 20–30 minutes until the oil and tomatoes separate. Remove from heat. Cook the spaghetti in plenty of salted boiling water until *al dente*. Meanwhile, drain most of the oil off the tuna, break it up with a fork and add to the tomato sauce. Drain the spaghetti and place in a serving bowl. Add half the tuna and tomato sauce and toss gently. Top with the remaining sauce, garnish with parsley and serve at once.

Pasta con Zucchini Fritti

The simple combination of spaghetti and lightly fried small courgettes provides another classic Sicilian pasta dish.

---

1 lb/450g small courgettes
½ tbsp salt
6 fl oz/175ml/¾ cup olive oil
1 tsp garlic, finely chopped
1 tbsp parsley, finely chopped
1 lb/450g spaghetti
25g/1oz butter
freshly ground black pepper
freshly grated Parmesan cheese
a few basil leaves

Wash and trim the courgettes and slice into discs ¼ inch/1 cm thick. Put them in a colander, sprinkle with salt and leave to disgorge for up to 1 hour. Place the olive oil in a saucepan over a moderate heat. Pat dry the courgette slices and fry them in the oil until golden brown on both sides. When almost cooked, add the garlic and parsley. Remove from the pan and drain on absorbent paper. Reserve about 2–3 tablespoons of olive oil. Cook the spaghetti in plenty of salted, boiling water until *al dente*. Put the reserved oil, butter and pepper in a warmed serving dish. Add the drained spaghetti and half the fried courgettes and toss gently. Garnish with the remaining courgettes, Parmesan cheese and the basil and serve at once.

Pasta 'Ncasciata

'*Ncasciata* in Sicilian dialect means "encased" and in this spectacular dish, the aubergine forms a case for the other flavoursome ingredients. Traditionally made in a dome-shaped mould, this recipe works equally well in a springform cake tin.

---

2 large aubergines cut into ¼ inch/6mm slices
salt
tomato sauce (see p. 0)
vegetable oil for frying
1 lb/450g rigatoni or penne
2oz/50g butter
8oz/350g mozzarella cheese, chopped
10 tbsp freshly grated Parmesan or pecorino cheese
1 tbsp dried oregano
pepper
2 tbsp fresh white breadcrumbs

Place the slices of aubergine in a colander, sprinkle lightly with salt and set aside to drain for an hour. Prepare the tomato sauce as described for *Pasta alla Norma*. Heat the oil in a large frying pan and add the slices of aubergine a few at a time. Fry until golden brown and place on absorbent paper. Cook the rigatoni until *al dente* in plenty of salted boiling water. Drain, return to the pan and add the butter. Mix in the tomato sauce, the mozzarella, 8 tablespoons of Parmesan/pecorino, oregano and pepper. Pre-heat the oven to gas mark 5/375°F/190°C. Line the bottom and sides of an 8 inch/20cm springform tin with the slices of aubergine. Fill the tin with the tomato/rigatoni mixture and sprinkle the top with a mixture of breadcrumbs and the remaining Parmesan/pecorino. Bake for 20–25 minutes, unmould and serve at once.

Tonno in Agrodolce

Tuna fishing has been part of Sicilian life for centuries. The fish are caught in a series of nets and are then harpooned in *La Mattanza*, an ancient ritual of such brutality it inspired the Greek dramatist Aeschylus to compare it to the battle of Salamis. The Roman cookery writer Apicius gives a recipe for tuna in a sweet and sour sauce and this combination of flavours is still popular in contemporary Sicilian cooking. Obtaining good, fresh tuna is not possible everywhere. This recipe, however, works very well with frozen fish.

---

4 fresh or frozen tuna steaks	2 tsp granulated sugar
3oz/75g flour	3 tbsp red wine vinegar
4 tbsp olive oil	4 tbsp dry white wine
2 medium onions, finely sliced	2 tbsp parsley, finely chopped
salt and pepper	

Remove the skin from the tuna and toss the steaks in the flour. Put 2 tablespoons of olive oil in a large pan and add the onion. Cook over a gentle heat until the onions soften. Then raise the heat and fry them until they turn golden brown. Remove the onions from the pan and add the rest of the olive oil. When hot fry the tuna steaks for 2–3 minutes on both sides. Season them with salt and pepper. Put in the sugar, vinegar, wine and onions. Cover the pan and cook over a high heat for a further 2–3 minutes. Remove the lid, add the parsley, turn the steaks once or twice in the sauce and remove them from the pan. Pour the sauce over the tuna and serve at once.

Pescespada alla Ghiotta

Swordfish, like tuna, have been caught by Sicilian fishermen using a harpoon in a tradition which dates back to Greek and Roman times. When fresh, swordfish steaks are at their best marinated in oil, lemon juice and herbs – a *salmoriglio* – and then grilled. This recipe, however, works equally well with fresh or frozen fish. *Ghiotta* originally referred to a type of pan but when used to describe a dish, indicates a sauce which is rich and full of flavour.

---

8 tbsp olive oil
1 onion, finely chopped
14oz/400g tin chopped tomatoes
4oz/100g capers, chopped
4oz/100g pitted green olives, chopped
4 swordfish steaks
salt and pepper

Put the oil and the finely chopped onion in a frying pan and sauté until the onion is golden. Add the chopped tomatoes and cook over a medium heat for 15–20 minutes until the sauce is reduced. Add the capers and olives and simmer for a few more minutes. Put the swordfish steaks in an ovenproof dish, pour the sauce over them and bake in a moderate oven at gas mark 4/350°F/180°C for 10–15 minutes until the steaks are cooked through. Potatoes, boiled or sautéed go well with this dish.

Sarde al Beccaficu

This sardine dish is so named because when cooked the fish are said to look like *beccafichi* – little birds. The stuffing of raisins and pine nut shows yet again the Arab influence on the food of the island.

4oz/100g breadcrumbs	12 bay leaves
2 tbsp olive oil	juice of 1 orange
4 anchovy fillets, chopped	juice of 1 lemon
2oz/50g raisins	1 tsp sugar
2oz/50g pine nuts	salt and freshly ground pepper
12 whole sardines	

Pre-heat the oven to gas mark 4/350°F/180°C. Toast the breadcrumbs in a frying pan over a moderate heat, stirring constantly to prevent them from sticking. As soon as they are golden, mix in one tablespoon of olive oil, chopped anchovy fillets, raisins, pine nuts and a little salt, then set aside. Cut the heads off the sardines, clean and fillet them but leave their tails on. Flatten the sardines with the palm of your hand and pat them dry with absorbent paper. Put a spoonful of the breadcrumb mixture on the wide end of each sardine and roll them up towards the tail. Pack them tightly in a greased, ovenproof dish, allowing the tails to stick up. Intersperse each sardine with a whole by leaf. Spoon the orange and lemon juice together with the remaining olive oil over the sardines and season with salt and pepper. Bake in the oven for 15 minutes. Serve at room temperature.

Braciolettine

For centuries meat was a luxury rarely enjoyed by Sicilian peasants. With a little meat and a lot of imagination the island's inventive cooks created *braciolettine* now found in various guises all over Sicily. Each region has its own variation. This recipe comes from Palermo.

---

1 medium onion, finely chopped
4oz/100g breadcrumbs
2oz/50g pecorino cheese, grated
2oz/50g raisins
2oz/50g pine nuts
2 large ripe tomatoes, peeled and chopped
salt and pepper
1 lb/400g topside of beef, thinly sliced and cut into 3 inch/7½ cm squares
4oz/100g fresh cacciocavallo or mozzarella cheese
2oz/50g salami, thinly sliced
bay leaves
oil

Fry the onion until soft. Remove from heat and add breadcrumbs, pecorino cheese, raisins, pine nuts and tomatoes. Season with salt and pepper, mix thoroughly and place one tablespoon of the mixture on to each square of beef. Add a cube of cheese and a slice of salami. Roll up the squares of meat and thread them on to skewers together with a bay leaf. Brush the meat with oil and cook over a barbecue or under a hot grill until the meat is cooked.

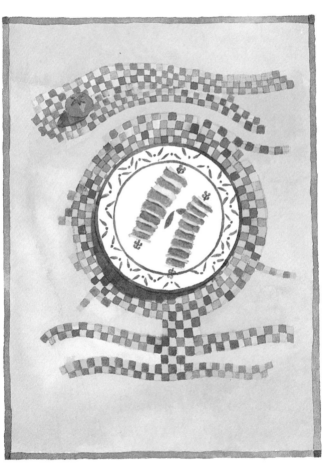

Farsumagru

The name of this dish literally means "false lean" and consists of a piece of lean beef filled with a very rich stuffing. Probably inspired by the more humble *bracciolone*, this is the version French chefs or *monsus* (the local version of *monsieur*) served to their wealthy, Sicilian aristocrat employers.

1 ½ lb/700g slice of topside of beef	1 egg
12oz/350g fairly fatty pork, minced	salt and freshly ground black pepper
2 tbsp parsley, finely chopped	3 tbsp flour
1 clove garlic, finely chopped	2 tbsp olive oil
2 tbsp fresh breadcrumbs	1 oz/25g butter
2 tbsp Parmesan cheese, freshly grated	5 tbsp/75ml red wine
	1 tbsp tomato purée
	2 fl oz/60ml/¼ cup warm water

Flatten the steak into a rectangular shape until ½ inch/1 ¼ cm thick. Fold the slice of meat in two, and using a trussing needle and fine string, sew up two of the sides to form a pocket. Combine the minced pork, parsley, garlic, breadcrumbs, cheese and egg in a bowl. Add salt and pepper to taste and mix together. Stuff the pocket of the meat with this mixture and sew up the remaining opening. Toss the meat parcel in the flour. Heat the oil and butter in a lidded sauté pan. When the butter foams, put in the meat roll and brown it all over. Add the red wine and reduce by half. Then put in the tomato purée and when it dissolves, pour in the water. Reduce the heat under the sauté pan to medium-low and cook on a gentle simmer for 1 ½ hours turning the meat roll from time to time. When cooked, cut the *farsumagru* in slices and lay them on a serving dish. Spoon over the sauce and serve at once.

Pollo alla Messinese

Sicilian meat and poultry dishes, for many centuries eaten only by the rich, tend to be elaborate and blanketed in well-flavoured sauces. Here, a simple chicken is transformed into a memorable dish with the addition of a sauce which uses some of the island's favourite ingredients.

---

1 3lb/1.5 kg chicken
1 stick celery
a few sprigs of parsley and basil
4oz/100g tinned tuna
1 tbsp capers
4 anchovy fillets
3/4 pt/450ml/1 1/2 cup good mayonnaise
salt and pepper to taste
slices of lemon, olives and capers to garnish

Put the chicken in a large lidded saucepan, add the celery and herbs and enough water to cover it completely. Bring to the boil, put on the lid and let it simmer for 1 1/2 hours until it is thoroughly cooked. Leave the chicken to cool in its liquid. Flake the tuna and chop the capers and anchovies. Stir them into the mayonnaise. Carve the cooled chicken and arrange it on a serving dish. Cover with the mayonnaise mixture and decorate with slices of lemon, olives and capers.

Timballo di Maccheroni Bianco

"The burnished gold of the crusts, the fragrance of sugar and cinnamon they exuded, were but preludes to the delights released from the interior when the knife broke the crust." So Lampedusa in his novel *Il Gattopardo* lovingly describes the *timballo* served at Prince Fabrizio's table. This less elaborate version of one of Sicily's most baroque dishes nonetheless reflects the *cucina baronale* so beloved of the island's aristocracy.

Pasta Frolla:

9oz/250g plain flour	2oz/50g caster sugar
4oz/125g butter	pinch of salt
2 egg yolks	1 egg, beaten, to glaze

Combine the flour with the butter, egg, sugar and salt to form a dough. Wrap in cling film and chill.

For the filling:

2oz/50g dried porcini mushrooms	salt and pepper
1/2 onion, finely chopped	3oz/75g butter
4 tbsp oil	1 lb/400g penne
tomato paste	3oz/75g Parmesan cheese
8oz/250g chicken livers	4oz/100g ham, thickly sliced
1/2 glass white wine	and cut into strips

Soak the dried mushrooms in enough warm water to cover for up to half an hour. Sauté the onion in a little olive oil until soft. Add the tomato paste and cook for a couple of minutes. Put in the chicken livers and fry lightly until they are coloured. Pour in the white wine, add the mushrooms and the water in which they were soaked. Cook on a moderate heat for about 20 minutes, and at the end of the cooking time add half the butter to the sauce. Season with salt and pepper.

Cook the penne in plenty of salted boiling water until *al dente*. Drain and mix with the rest of the butter, the grated Parmesan cheese, the ham and the mushroom/liver sauce.

Oil an 8 inch/20 cm springform cake tin and line the base and sides with two-thirds of the *pasta frolla*. Fill the pastry case with the penne mixture pressing it down firmly. Cover with the rest of the pastry and brush with the beaten egg. Bake in a moderate oven at gas mark 4/350°F/180°C for about 30 minutes. Let the *timballo* rest for 5 minutes before releasing it from the tin. Cut into wedges and serve.

Frittedda

Eaten only in the spring when the peas, beans and artichokes are young and tender, a *frittedda* exemplifies the Sicilian genius for cooking vegetables. Frozen or tinned vegetables may be used in this recipe, but the results are not so good.

---

6 artichokes	6oz/150g peas (shelled weight)
1 medium onion, finely chopped	10 fl oz/250ml/1 cup water
6 tbsp olive oil	salt and freshly ground
6oz/150g broad beans	black pepper
(shelled weight)	

First prepare the artichokes. Have ready a bowl of acidulated water and begin by removing the tough, outer leaves of the artichoke, cutting off the stalk and trimming the top. Cut the artichoke

in half, remove the furry choke and plunge what remains briefly into the water. Then sauté the onion in the olive oil until soft. Add the beans and cook for three minutes. Cut the artichokes into quarters and add to the beans. Cook for a further 3 minutes, then add the peas, fresh water, salt and pepper. Cover and cook for 20–25 minutes or until the artichokes are tender. Serve warm or cold.

Caponata

Aubergines arrived in Sicily with the Arab invaders and are now used endlessly in the island's cooking. The sweet and sour flavour of this vegetable stew makes it a typically Sicilian dish.

---

4 medium aubergines, cubed	salt and pepper
5 tbsp olive oil	1 tbsp capers
1 onion, finely sliced	4 sticks of celery finely sliced
14oz/400g tin chopped	2oz/50g pitted green olives
tomatoes or 6 fresh tomatoes,	4 tbsp wine vinegar
skinned and chopped	1 tbsp sugar

Sprinkle the aubergines with salt and allow to disgorge for half an hour or so. Pat dry, fry in 4 tablespoons of the olive oil until golden brown and then leave to drain on absorbent paper. Gently fry the onion in one tablespoon of olive oil until golden. Add the tomatoes and salt and cook until the sauce thickens. Put in the capers, celery and olives, and cook for another 10–15 minutes until the celery softens. Add the cooked aubergines to the sauce with the vinegar and sugar. Cook over a low heat until the vinegar evaporates. Allow the mixture to cool, and serve as part of an *antipasto* or as a side dish.

Melanzane alla Parmigiana

Contrary to what its name suggests, this dish is Sicilian in origin and is found in various guises all over the island.

---

4 large aubergines
oil for frying
1 medium onion, finely chopped
4 cloves garlic
2 14oz/400g tins chopped tomatoes
1 tsp sugar
salt and pepper to taste.
a handful of basil leaves, roughly torn
4oz/100g Parmesan cheese, freshly grated

Slice the aubergines into rounds, place in a colander, sprinkle with salt and leave to disgorge for about an hour. Sweat the onion and the garlic in a little oil and add the tomatoes, the sugar, salt and pepper. Cook over a medium heat until the sauce is thick and glossy. Heat 1/2 inch/1 cm of the oil in a large frying pan and when it is very hot add the slices of aubergine and fry until they are golden brown, then drain on absorbent paper. Pre-heat the oven to gas mark 4/375°F/180°C. Cover the bottom of a gratin dish with a little of the tomato sauce. Place the slices of aubergine in the gratin dish, cover with tomato sauce, basil leaves and grated Parmesan. Repeat this process until all the aubergine is used up, finishing with a generous layer of Parmesan. Bake in the oven for about 20 minutes. Serve at room temperature.

Broccoli con Olive Nere

For Sicilians, broccoli is a kind of green cauliflower and is used a great deal in pasta dishes, in salads and as a vegetable.

---

2 heads green cauliflower (2 lb/900g)
4 fl oz/¹/₂ cup olive oil
1 onion, very finely chopped
4 oz/100g/¹/₂ cup pitted black olives, sliced
4 oz/100g/¹/₂ cup Parmesan or pecorino cheese, grated
8oz/200g/1 cup mozzarella cheese, cubed

Cut the cauliflower into florets and blanch in salted boiling water for about 5 minutes, then drain and set aside. Put half the olive oil into a frying pan and add the onion to it. Sauté for a few minutes until the onion colours, add the olives, mix together and remove pan from the heat. Pre-heat the oven to gas mark 4/375°F/180°C. Put the cauliflower in a greased ovenproof dish and mix with the onion and olives. Add the rest of the olive oil and season with salt and freshly ground black pepper. Sprinkle half the Parmesan over the vegetables and mix thoroughly. Scatter the cubes of mozzarella over the top and then sprinkle the remaining Parmesan over this. Bake for about 20 minutes or until there is a golden crust over the top. Serve warm.

Carciofi alle Mandorle

Like so much else in Sicilian food, artichokes were brought to the island by the Arabs and the word *carciofi* comes from the Arabic *al kharsuf*. Artichokes are prepared in numerous ways all over Sicily and this recipe uses an interesting mix of flavours, including almonds which were also brought by the conquering Arabs. Fresh globe artichokes are used here but good tinned artichoke hearts make a very acceptable substitute.

---

6 artichokes	4 tbsp olive oil
1 small onion, finely chopped	1 tbsp white wine vinegar
2 cloves garlic, crushed	juice of one lemon
3 anchovies, chopped	1 tbsp sugar
4oz/100g ground almonds	2 tbsp capers, chopped
1/2 pt/300ml/1 cup chicken stock	salt and pepper

Prepare the artichokes as described in the recipe for *Frittedda* (see p. 32). Set the hearts aside. Fry the onion and garlic in 1 tablespoon of the olive oil until they are golden. Add the anchovies, breaking them up with a spoon, then add the ground almonds and the chicken stock. Simmer for about 15 minutes until the mixture is thick and creamy. Beat in the oil, vinegar, lemon juice, sugar, salt and pepper and set aside to cool. Arrange the artichoke hearts in a serving dish and spoon the sauce over them. Garnish with the chopped capers. Serve cold.

Peperoni Arrostiti

Peperoni, sweet or bell peppers, were probably introduced to Sicily by the Spanish and unlike the tomato were quickly incorporated into the Sicilian diet. Jewel bright mounds of green, yellow and red peppers make a spectacular sight in Sicilian markets and in restaurants no *antipasto* selection is complete without roasted peppers. Sun-ripened Sicilian peppers, even green ones, are wonderfully sweet and tender. Their northern glasshouse grown cousins are less flavoursome, so for this recipe only yellow or red peppers should be used.

6 red or yellow sweet or bell peppers or a mixture of both	3–4 anchovy fillets
	1 clove garlic, peeled
olive oil	salt and pepper

Cut the peppers into quarters, remove the seeds and white membrane. Put on a rack under a pre-heated grill and cook until the skin is black and blistered. Remove from heat and put the peppers into a bowl, cover with cling film and leave to cool. Once cold the skin will slip easily from the peppers. Place the peeled peppers in a flat dish, pour on enough olive oil to cover, add the anchovy fillets, garlic, salt and pepper. Leave in a cool place and allow flavours to develop. Serve as a salad or part of an *antipasto*.

Insalata di Pomodoro e Cipolla

Though the Spanish probably brought the tomato to Sicily in the sixteenth century, it was regarded for some time with great suspicion and it was not until the eighteenth century that the Sicilian passion for the tomato began. They are now a central ingredient in everyday cooking.

---

8 flavoursome, ripe tomatoes, thinly sliced
1 red onion, peeled and thinly sliced
grated rind and juice of 1 lemon

2 tbsp olive oil
pinch of dried oregano
salt and freshly ground black pepper

Put the tomatoes in a flat dish. Lay the onion on top, sprinkle with the lemon rind and drizzle on the oil and lemon juice. Add the oregano, salt and pepper. Serve with lots of bread to mop up all the oil and juices.

Insalata di Arance e Olive Nere

This salad, North African in origin, is usually served before dessert or, in a more elaborate meal, as refreshment for flagging palates.

·4 large or 8 small seedless oranges
1 red onion

4oz/100g pitted black olives
olive oil
salt and pepper

Remove all the skin and pith from the oranges and slice thinly into rounds. Peel the onion and slice finely into rings. Combine the orange slices, onion rings and olives in a bowl. Add enough olive oil to coat the oranges and sprinkle with salt and freshly ground black pepper. Toss the salad gently and serve at once.

Pane Rimacinato

The Greeks and Romans both colonised Sicily and under their rule the island's fertile soil was cultivated to produce grain. The reverence the Sicilians feel for bread is undimmed. The flour used to make Sicilian bread, *Pane Rimacinato*, is durum wheat or semolina flour which has been twice milled. In appearance it is very fine, golden and silky to the touch and the bread made from it is pale yellow in colour with a crisp nut brown crust. This recipe makes two loaves and any left-overs can be used to make breadcrumbs.

---

5 tsp dried yeast granules
1 tsp sugar
1–1¼ pt/600–750ml/2–3 cups lukewarm water
2¼ lb/1 kg semolina or durum wheat flour
1 tbsp salt
2 tbsp/¼ cup olive oil

Dissolve the yeast granules and sugar in 8 fl oz/250ml/1 cup luke-warm water and leave for 15 minutes until it has developed a foam.

Put the flour and salt into a large bowl and make a well in the centre. Pour the yeast mixture into the well and using your hands gradually draw the rest of the flour into the middle of the bowl until the flour and yeast mixture are well mixed. Add the remaining water a little at a time, constantly working the dough until all the water has been absorbed. Now place the dough on a flat work surface and knead for 15–20 minutes. During the last few minutes of kneading add two tablespoons of olive oil to the dough. When ready it should be smooth and elastic. Form into two loaves and place on a floured baking sheet. Cover with a cloth and leave in a warm place to rise until the surface of the loaves is covered in tiny cracks and they have doubled in size (45 minutes – 1 hour). Pre-heat the oven to gas mark 7/400°F/200°C and bake the bread for approximately 1 hour until golden brown and firm to the touch.

Sfincione

This is the Palermo version of pizza and is sold in bakers' shops and by street vendors. It calls for cacciocavallo cheese, but if this is not available, mozzarella may be used instead. Again, breadcrumbs feature in this recipe, this time as a topping for the *sfincione*.

For the pizza dough:

1oz/25g dried yeast granules
½–¾ pt/300–350ml/
1–1½ cups tepid water

¾ lb/300g/2½ cups flour
salt
1–2 tbsp olive oil

For the topping:

4oz/100g cacciocavallo or
mozzarella cheese, diced
8 anchovy fillets, cut into pieces
4 fl oz/125ml/½ cup passata
1 onion, finely sliced and
softened in olive oil

2oz/50g breadcrumbs toasted
in a frying pan with a little
olive oil until brown
1 tbsp dried oregano
olive oil

Dissolve the yeast in ¼ pint/130ml/⅔ cup tepid water and leave until foam develops. Meanwhile, combine the flour and salt in a bowl, make a well in the centre and pour in the yeast. Mix to form a dough and knead for 10–15 minutes incorporating the olive oil during the last 5 minutes. When the dough is smooth and elastic, shape it to fit onto a well-oiled baking tray 9" x 12"/ 23 x 30 cm. Now scatter the diced cheese over the pizza, pressing it down into the dough. Do the same with the anchovies, and then cover with

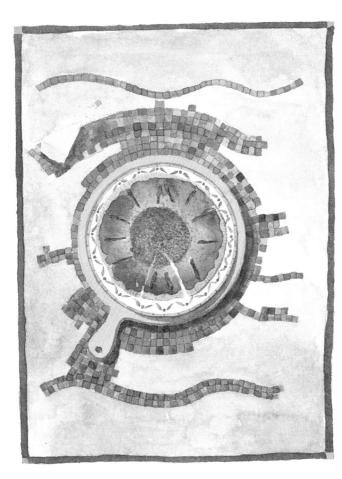

the passata and onions. Combine the breadcrumbs and the oregano and sprinkle them over the top. Drizzle some olive oil over the pizza and leave it somewhere warm and draught-free for about an hour until it rises. Pre-heat the oven to gas mark 7/425°F/ 220°C and bake the pizza for 30–40 minutes until the crust is brown and the topping crisp. Sprinkle with a little more olive oil, cut into squares and serve at once.

Formaggio all' Argentiera

History does not record the name of the Palermo silversmith who, according to legend, fell on hard times and invented this cheese dish as a substitute for fish or meat. We can only hope that he found a new career as a chef, because this simple recipe is an inspired creation.

---

4 tbsp olive oil
2 cloves garlic, peeled
I lb/450g cacciocavallo cheese (if not available, use provolone)
cut into slices ½ inch/2 cm thick
I tbsp wine vinegar
a good pinch of oregano

Put the olive oil and the cloves of garlic in a heavy pan over medium heat and cook until the garlic turns golden brown. Discard the garlic and add the slices of cheese. Fry until lightly browned on both sides. Add the vinegar and sprinkle on the oregano. Serve at once as an *antipasto* or as a cheese course.

Cassata Siciliana

It is perhaps for its *dolci* that Sicily is best known. Of these it is *Cassata Siciliana*, ringed with *pasta reale* and decorated with gem-like glacé fruits, which is the crowning glory. Traditionally an Easter treat, it is now eaten all through the year. Marsala, perhaps the best known of Sicilian wines is used in the recipe but any sweet liqueur can be substituted.

12oz/300g sponge cake, thinly sliced	few drops of vanilla extract
3–4 tbsp Marsala or sweet liqueur to taste (optional)	4oz/100g glacé fruit, chopped
	2oz/50g bitter chocolate, chopped
1 lb/500g ricotta cheese	2oz/50g marzipan, thinly rolled
4oz/100g caster sugar	4oz/100g glacé fruits, to decorate

Fondant icing:

12oz/300g icing sugar	lemon juice

Line the sides and bottom of an 8 inch/20 cm mould or springform tin with foil. Put in a layer of sponge and sprinkle with half the Marsala. Blend together the ricotta, caster sugar and vanilla extract. Stir in the chopped glacé fruit and bitter chocolate. Spoon the mixture into the mould and top with the remaining sponge cake. Sprinkle with the rest of the Marsala, cover with foil and refrigerate for a few hours. Turn the *cassata* out onto a plate. Cover the sides of the cake with the marzipan, leaving the top exposed. To prepare the fondant icing, combine the sugar with enough lemon juice to produce a spreading consistency, adding a little water if necessary to give a smooth, shiny appearance. Ice the top of the *cassata*, decorate with glacé fruits and refrigerate until ready to serve.

Cannoli

Cannoli are part of Sicily's ancient tradition of pastry and sweet making. Sicilians buy their *cannoli* at the local bakery, but they are so delicious it is worth trying to make them at home, though you will require *cannoli* tubes to shape them.

1 tbsp butter	1 tbsp Marsala
4oz/100g plain flour	vegetable oil for frying
1 tbsp cocoa powder	2oz/50g pistachio nuts,
1 tsp caster sugar	finely chopped
pinch of salt	icing sugar

Rub the butter into the flour, add the cocoa powder, sugar, salt and marsala. Knead the pastry for about 15 minutes, adding more wine if necessary until it is smooth and elastic like a pasta dough. Roll the pastry as thinly as possible, using a pasta machine if available. Using a saucer cut into rounds which fit around the *cannoli* tube. Seal the edges with a little water. In a large saucepan heat 2–3 inches/5–7 1/2 cm oil and when ready, fry the *cannoli* until dark brown, 1–2 minutes. Drain on absorbent paper and when cool, slide them off their tubes.

Ricotta Cream

8oz/250g ricotta	2oz/50g chocolate, chopped
4oz/100g caster sugar	1oz/25g candied peel, chopped
a few drops vanilla extract	

Combine the ricotta, sugar and vanilla extract in a bowl and blend until smooth. Stir in the chocolate and the candied peel. Use this mixture to stuff the *cannoli*, sprinkle with chopped pistachio nuts and dredge with the sugar.

Gelato di Pistachio

Whatever the origins of ice cream, by the eleventh century, the Arab rulers had introduced *sarbat*, a frozen drink of milk and honey, to Sicily. From this comes the word *sorbet* and the Sicilians' strong claim for developing the milk-based product we know as ice cream. *Gelaterie* in Sicily offer a dazzling array of flavours but one of the most striking and typical of the island is pistachio ice cream. Please note that this recipe requires an ice cream maker.

1³/4 pt/1 ltr/5 cups milk	2oz/50g ground almonds
12oz/360g caster sugar	4oz/100g pistachio nuts, shelled,
4 tbsp cornflour	peeled and finely ground
a few drops of vanilla extract	
or essence	

Heat 1¹/2 pints/900ml/3³/4 cups of the milk with the sugar until they reach boiling point. Mix the cornflour with the remaining milk and add to the milk and sugar. Return to boiling point, stirring constantly until mixture begins to thicken slightly and then remove from heat. Add a few drops of the vanilla extract or essence and leave to cool. When cold, add the ground almonds and pistachio nuts and following manufacturers' instructions churn in an ice cream maker. When the mixture has reached the right consistency, transfer to a container and freeze. Before serving, allow the ice cream to ripen in the refrigerator for at least half an hour.

Torta di Ricotta

Ricotta cheese, almonds, honey and lemon are ingredients typical of many Sicilian desserts. Here they are combined to produce a delicately flavoured dessert which captures the very essence of Sicilian sweets.

10oz/300g shortcrust pastry	3 tbsp caster sugar
3oz/75g unblanched almonds	zest of 1 lemon, finely grated
1 lb/450g ricotta cheese	juice of 1 lemon
3 eggs, separated	2 tbsp icing sugar
5 tbsp clear honey	

Roll out the pastry and line a 9 inch/23 cm tart tin (preferably with a removable base). Rest in the refrigerator for about 30 minutes.

Pre-heat the oven to gas mark 5/375°F/190°C. Bake the pastry case blind for 15 minutes and set aside to cool. Finely grind the almonds in a food processor. Beat together the ricotta, egg yolks, honey, sugar, lemon zest and juice, and the ground almonds until well mixed. Whisk the egg whites until they are stiff, but not dry, and fold them into the mixture. Spoon the filling into the pastry case and bake at gas mark 4/350°F/180°C for about 35 minutes until the top is light gold and firm to the touch. Leave the tart to cool and then refrigerate for a couple of hours. Dust lightly with the sugar before serving.

Index